I0558291

Consistency

How Small Daily Actions Shape the Way to a Fruitful Lifestyle

(Achieving Your Goals through Persistence Mastering the Art of Consistency in Fitness)

Marcos Parker

Published By **Andrew Zen**

Marcos Parker

All Rights Reserved

Consistency: How Small Daily Actions Shape the Way to a Fruitful Lifestyle (Achieving Your Goals through Persistence Mastering the Art of Consistency in Fitness)

ISBN   978-1-9995502-0-2

Legal & Disclaimer

Table Of Contents

Chapter 1: Our Attitude and What We Tell Ourselves

Prior to implementing changes in our routines every day one of the most crucial change that we must to address is self-talk as well as the attitude. When I do a check-in with my clients about the changes they've made after our last meeting what they typically discuss is the few things that they think they've missed. They are completely unaware of the things they could have done better.

If we're making modifications to our lives it's crucial to acknowledge your successes as well as be able to learn from our mistakes. Though I understand the necessity to keep track of the mistakes and difficulties someone experienced that were not successful, if you solely concentrate on the negative outcomes, you'll be being overwhelmed, angry and will often stop pursuing the goals you set.

Take the moment each day to reflect on your accomplishments to get closer to your goals. Small changes, like eating smaller portions of your favorite food served for the potluck or putting the time for a walk of 10 minutes between when your child needs to attend school for rehearsal and the time you start the concert, these tiny victories will add up the same as (if less than) those that fail and only if you acknowledge yourself for the accomplishments.

If mistakes or challenges occur that create problems keep in mind that there's nothing called failing, but rather the opportunity to grow. The only way to fail is in the event that you do not master the skills to be succeed next time, or if you cease your quest totally. Take the lessons learned from your mistakes or failures, and move towards success.

That's what I am referring to when I refer to Consistent Persistence. There are always roadblocks and hurdles in pursuit of any objective. The most important thing is to never let them hinder your efforts. Making consistent progress towards the goal can ultimately lead you to your goal and allow you to maintain your goal in mind, no matter the amount of detours in the process.

Another crucial aspect of our mindset is what you are saying to you about yourself? In the course of our week, we are engaged in numerous conversations with ourselves about various issues. It's important to ensure that your conversations with yourself feel as positive energy boost rather than an uplifting pep talk instead of a take-down after put-down. It is simple to determine the fact that what you're telling yourself is more of negative or a slur through asking yourself "Would I be ok with someone else saying this about me?"

It's all about embracing it, not accepting the fact that it's happening. A lot of us have put ourselves down for such a long time that whenever we hear about it from other people that we can accept it but it doesn't mean that you're okay with the fact that it's happening! We can become accustomed to accepting negative comments, yet experiencing a sense of loss each whenever you hear the word.

There are a myriad of theories, like The Law of Attraction or self-fulfilling prophecy that shows our beliefs about ourselves more is the most likely to show up within our daily lives. Take a moment to consider whether you are spending all time telling yourself things that are negative such as:

* "I'm fat."

* "I'm not worth it."

* "I'll never be able to do something like that."

If you don't it, you'll expose yourself to others in the hope that they are seeing what you're saying to yourself. The thoughts we think about can influence the perceptions that other people have of us, which causes how they interact with us to reflect their views. It's like a complete circle since we can see from others' behavior toward us, that what we've believed to be true is real.

Cycle of Self-Talk

This is the right moment to be in control of altering the way that we speak about us. If someone were talking to you in a negative way frequently then you'd probably quit being friends with them, would you not? One common error individuals make while trying to change negative self-talk into positive self-talk is to concentrate on things they don't want instead of what we actually want. Example:

* "I won't be nervous and miss out on what I want."

* "I don't want to feel worthless."

* "I won't make unhealthy choices today."

It's difficult to focus on what we don't wish to be in the present. Instead, think about your focus on what you desire to be or achieve. When you are focused on your goals the self-talk you use will gain the power to be more powerful.

If you have things that you wish people would tell to you more frequently, begin telling yourself these items. It is now clear the process of getting rid of the habit of self-defeating will not be easy. Whatever way other people take care of you, you're always in control of what you tell yourself.

The thing I would recommend doing during the day is anytime you feel stuck in a downward spiral Find something positive and encouraging to say to yourself. It's called positive affirmation. Positive affirmations are the shortest form of affirmation you will repeat to yourself in confidence. A few examples are:

* "I am confident and successful in everything I do."

* "I am worthy of being happy in life."

* "I am healthier every day."

It's important to tailor the affirmation, not just to things you want and want, but affirm it as authentic. It isn't effective when you instantly afterward, you repeat the affirmation with self-talk that is negative. Affirmations must be spoken in the present, as like you are already the things you are. It's just there to help you remember. The repetition of affirmations with the present tense reduces your ability to live in the present and here and now.

Positive affirmations are great to utilize at the beginning of the day, to establish an positive outlook to your daily routine. Additionally, you may utilize affirmations throughout the important phases of the day, like moments of tension, conflict or any other time where you are aware that you'll have to take an informed decision.

Take some of the affirmations you make by placing them in a place in which you will be able to view the positive thoughts in the forefront of your thoughts. This could be at the mirror in your bathroom as well as your fridge, driver's dashboard, on the display screen for your lock or the home screen on your phone, as well as on your office desk or at work. As you continue to see and repeat these thoughts to yourself as you go, the more these messages will become a part of your subconscious and replace the negative ones.

Another two ideas are using journaling. The first one is an Thankfulness Journal. It is usually used towards the end of your day as an opportunity to reflect upon the things you're grateful for during the day.

This is a way to take your mind off all negative and negative issues and allow yourself to acknowledge all the positive moments that took place this day. You are welcome to recognize those things that were wrong, or simply bad However, focusing in the negative can be a distraction from the negativities.

It's known as frequency illusion. It's also called"the blue car" theory. The blue car theory occurs that you or somebody you know purchases the blue car when suddenly, wherever you are, the only thing you can notice is blue vehicles. The mind is always looking for what we focus our attention to. If events don't turn out the way you'd like them to consider taking a second to re-evaluate your viewpoint. Do you think that you are only looking at the negative aspect? Do you see anything positive in this incident? If the experience was truly terrible, think about the lessons you could have learned from the experience - so that you're able to make improvements and get more prepared the next time that a similar scenario occurs - then proceed to the next one.

Chapter 2: The Meaning of Our Words

We would like to take the time now to consider words and their meanings, as well as the differences in the definition of words and what our unconscious meaning tells us. Like the importance of self-talk positive and the impact it has on our attitude and motivations as well, the words we speak as well as the meaning behind them could have the same effect.

My most favorite word in this topic can be "try." The definition of"try" is the act of making an effort. It doesn't mean the ability to achieve success, an objective, or overcome a problem. A lot of times, people tell me that they strive to accomplish something in pursuit of their intention, and frequently If I don't focus to change their words in order to clarify their motivations toward their goals, what they will tell me the every time I talk to them is that they have tried to reach their goal, only to be interrupted by the word "but." This "but" could be an excuse or reason why they aren't reaching their goals. Example "I tried to exercise three days this week, but I couldn't make it to the gym on Wednesday because of traffic."

The most important issue is how initially the words we choose to use in setting goals have upon our minds. When somebody says they will try to accomplish things, they're saying to themselves and other people that they will work hard towards achieving the goal but that things are likely hinder their progress or stop the effort from being achieved. When we declare an objective - "I will do this" ..."" - we're affirming to ourselves and other people that I will accomplish this goal and over come any obstacles might get between me and my goal. In the end, Yoda said it best, "Do or do not, there is no try."

Another word that I often hear in the face of problems can be "can't." Whenever you are tempted to use "I can't" to explain the reason you're not taking action it is my suggestion to consider asking yourself "Is it really can't, or is it won't?" The term "can" used in "can't" is a reference to the capacity to perform anything. "Can" is a reference to having the ability to do something "will" is the root of "won't," which refers to the will to bring the desired outcome. If we claim that you can't perform anything, i.e., exercise is it a sign we don't have the capacity to exercise? Do we actually mean that we don't have the motivation to achieve it? The distinction between getting results or not achieving your goals often is in the ability to overcome or be defeated by challenges that arise within your own daily life.

The discussion of can't versus will't brings us to a second major word related to bringing about life-style changes that is motivation. Motivation can be defined as the overall desire or determination for someone to take action. It is important to have motivation integral to you in order to implement modifications to your life Motivation is among the top five motives I've observed for people to choose to hire personal trainers. Motivation is tied to two additional key behavioral aspects such as responsibility and procrastination.

The concept of accountability is to follow through on objectives we have set for yourself when we feel driven. However, there are instances when motivation may slide - be it the temptation to indulge in unhealthy food or the desire to devote time somewhere other than at the gym. Being accountable can go a long way in ensuring that you keep the fire of motivation burning. It's much simpler to refuse the extra portion or to keep the gym schedule with an accountability partner outside of your own. No matter if you're working with a close friend as an accountability buddy or someone who is a professional in full, having an ongoing check-in is the key to achieving the target.

The act of procrastination is the death of motivation. Think about how many times did you put off starting your fitness routine or diet with the excuse, "I'll start it Monday," in order to wait for an event occur that makes you justification yourself that, "I'll start it next week." In the end you'll realize that it's been a whole year in "next weeks." No anyone is safe from the wrath of delay - as an example to be honest, my original draft for this book was written in 2008!

If we talk about procrastination or motivation I am often reminded of the interview I saw some time ago on The Steve Harvey Show talking to Eric Thomas. Eric Thomas made the comment that he didn't think that procrastination is a good thing. Thomas explained that matters are either significant to you, or they're not. The degree of importance determines whether it's important enough for you to set aside to it. His remarks were not a the context of a student who was struggling to finish school I have seen this happen every time prospective clients seek help.

Many of us delay making any changes to our diet and exercise until we've got a terrible appointment with a doctor.

Cholesterol and high blood pressure diabetes and various other ailments are all a reason for excess storage of fat due to unhealthy diets and lack of exercise. Yet, regardless of that, many people hold off on increasing their exercise and implementing healthier eating habits until the bad test results is revealed. It's now the time to make it a priority since your whole life depends on the results. In the end, once you've reached this level that more radical fitness and nutrition changes will be required, while if you decide to become more healthy now, fewer significant changes will be required simply since it's much more simple to keep your health in good shape as opposed to gaining it back.

A third factor that influences motivation, and how to keep it going is the concept of momentum. Many people consider momentum an actual physical force. Yet, very few are aware of the concept of momentum to be a psychological force also.

It is possible that you are familiar with Newton's Law of physics which states that objects will remain in motion or at rest until it is impacted by a larger force outside. The concept of mental momentum is regarded as a force within the body in the sense that the object is the person you are.

If we're looking to make modifications in our lives or just trying to push ourselves further and reach the next level of our efficiency, mental energy is what makes us effective. If you've had the urge to accomplish something and then resisted it by stating multiple reasons to stop it You're aware of the concept of mental momentum. It's a force which could either hold us in a stalemate and hinder us from progressing but it also can propel us to achieve greater and more impressive things.

The trick is to get the mental energy to work to benefit you. Concentrating on positive self-talk, instead of negative self-talk is one approach. Instead of dwelling on the reasons you won't, or can't accomplish something, think of the small thing that you are able to accomplish and then the advantages that come from it. If you're concerned about performing, imagine yourself as success instead of being unsuccessful. People often get sucked into a state of paralysis of analysis and allow our thoughts spin over possibilities of how things might be a disaster. If you are unable to imagine yourself doing something and you don't believe that it will succeed. Make small adjustments If big changes are too daunting:

* A positive reflection about your self is great considering that everything that you've told yourself about yourself has been negative until this point.

5 minutes of walking is far better than no walk in any way.

* Making a change to one portion of your diet each week for a healthier diet is a great beginning.

Find at least every day a positive thing instead of focusing on things that aren't so good.

A small step towards self-improvement is better than remaining at the same level. Making the shift to focus on the positive is the initial stage to establishing healthier habit. The phrases we choose to use are important to us so much.

Our Perceptions and Their Impact

One of the main factors that influences the way we talk is how we interpret the happenings within our daily lives. Every event is neutral. But it's only after we assign the events a name like negative or positive based on the values we hold and our past events that they acquire an identity.

As a simple example In any sports event, there's an winner and a loser. If this is a positive or negative thing is dependent on the team you're supporting. It's really just an event, however when your team is winning, it's thrilling. But if the team's losing and you're disappointed, then it's frustrating.

It is evident that everything depends on perception. Therefore, in everyday circumstances such as traffic, weather and computer problems, etc. These are neutral, and are not requiring the triggering of a powerful emotional response. It is more important to have the ability to control and moderate your choice of reaction. If you spend the day constantly reacting angry emotions in response to events which occur, it's likely that you will end up feeling overwhelmed, irritable and emotionally exhausted.

Instead of operating in an autopilot that is emotionally reactive and often resulting in the crash, think about taking a deliberate decision about the way you react to be during each scenario. One of the most important things to consider at every moment is "Will this have any further need of my attention or greater impact on my life?"

Traffic delays and being stranded, or someone who doesn't respond to your greetings on the street do not require the person to be emotionally connected to them for the rest throughout the entire day. If you've ever retell an incident to someone at the final moments of the day regarding what transpired in their morning commute is aware of the emotional attachment. If you are experiencing the same anxiety and emotional turmoil when you retell the story the story as if it happened and you're emotionally tied to the incident. From a perspective point of view, although it is possible to bring up an incident who cut you off on your commute to work, if they ask you immediately after you arrive at work, it is unlikely that you would mention it if it came up after getting back home.

It is therefore essential to determine if this incident is going to be relevant in five hours' time. If not let it go and stop thinking about it because every one of these chains either good or bad can be a lead jacket or metal chain or lead jacket hindering our ability to advance and securing us in an area, turning through circles, repeating this identical process over and over again, resulting in new attachments which bind us and limit us further.

This is the perfect moment to let go of the chains to remove the weights, and begin to take steps forward in your journey. The change you make, like other ones discussed is a gradual process. It isn't an instant success. This may cause more discontent and disappointment. It is important to recognize this event in a neutral way and then move on when it happens, and when you have made that deliberate decision. But, if it becomes apparent later on that you had an emotional bond with the reaction you made, you are able to after that moment of realizing, choose an entirely new choice to release the emotion and go on.

However, I'm not suggesting that there aren't likely to be situations that your reaction will be emotionally charged. Examples include breakups, being married, losing of a beloved one or even the birth of a baby can be majorly emotional moments that happen in our lives.

But, a lot of things that are considered to be undesirable or harmful are very likely to become another chain of emotions which impedes us and hinders our progress ahead. Take a look. What number of times have a program for exercise or diet been abandoned because we reverted to unhealthy snacks and eating, settling on the sofa slouch watching TV or scrolling away on our smartphones - simply because an unfortunate incident occurred, and our feelings become the main cause? And even after the fog of emotions begins to lift and we see how far back we've fallen in our self-talk, fueled by the fresh negativity will try to keep us glued to the unproductive behaviors that we have been avoiding:

* "See, I'll always be fat, because this is who I am."

* "No point in starting again, I'll just find another reason to quit anyways."

... as well as a lot of other negative thoughts and feelings that are weighing us down and preventing uns from making positive changes that we desire and need.

It is an important method to experience grieving, or release process for a variety of reasons but the goal should be being able to acknowledge and progress. If you are feeling dragged to the ground and stuck due to those negative thoughts and feelings that don't seem to be able to go away, I recommend seeking additional assistance. You can do this through help groups and life coaches, or even counseling.

The majority of employers offer the Employee Assistance Program (EAP) and can supply you with the names of therapists and counselors within the area you live in. Health and mental health are just equally important as your physical health, and if not more, since mental health is often linked to harmful habits and actions that affect the physical health of your. It's not wrong to consider getting help for your mental health. For instance, if could have a leg that continuously was walking backward each time you tried to go forward, then it would be advisable to see a doctor or physical therapist to get help isn't it?

The reason I am bringing this up is that often, our prior efforts to live a healthier life failed. If you are adamant about the "failures," that is that which you are most likely to do for you. Try to view them as just that - attempts that failed, but they taught you something from the experience. It is important to determine the obstacles that led to the loss.

Next, you must develop a strategy for what you will do to overcome any obstacles that may arise if they arise repeatedly. Instead of being the feeling of a "failure," you have been able to learn from your experience that allows you to better prepare for the future and achieve the ultimate goal.

Chapter 3: Goal Setting

Let's discuss goals. When setting goals for ourselves, a helpful tool is to follow the SMART (specific, measurable, attainable/achievable, relevant, time-based) format. Goals that are specific make it simpler to determine what exactly your plan should be to succeed. As an example:

* I will walk two days a week.

*I will include a vegetable serving in each meal.

Measurable objectives allow us to assess how well we've succeeded in achieving the objective. The process can be completed in a specific duration or time period, i.e. 20, 20 mins or a specific amount of days each week. Any measure which allows you to know how you compare to your goals is right.

It's crucial to set objectives that are achievable and meet. Like, for instance, setting the goal of losing weight to an amount you've never experienced since childhood might not be feasible. Importantly, it is important to set goals that are relevant to ensure that we don't get too focused on things that could hinder our larger goals. Making goals we've none of the means to achieve or establishing a deadline can result in despair, depression as well as, in the end, ending up in despair.

Goals based on time are crucial because they help us be accountable to the time we begin and to when we'd like the goals to be completed. If this is not in place, someone may be trying constantly to "exercise more," never being aware of when they will have completed the task, or even putting it off since there's no set date.

If you are creating goals, it's appropriate to have big objectives, like those previously mentioned in terms of nutrition and exercise, nevertheless, you should set smaller goals that aid you to reach your goals. The breaking down of big goals into smaller targets makes it easier to monitor progress and increase motivation after each achievement.

A different aspect to note when considering the goal setting process: you have examine the distinction between outcomes goals and process goals. The majority of the time, we will encounter outcomes goals, like winning a match or achieving a certain weight or reducing the time it takes to walk or run a mile. This can lead to disappointment or a lack of accomplishment as they are the result of other actions and they are not things we have any direct influence over.

Process goals However, they also are focused on our actions and decisions, like techniques we employ in a sport to become a better athlete as well as changes in nutrition and exercise to improve our health or running regularly to improve stamina and speed. You can clearly see that many of these goals are likely to achieve the intended effect on previous goals. The process goals, however, put your focus on the things you do with your day-to-day life. They give greater control over results and greater chances to achieve your goals.

Another advantage to focusing on goals for process rather than only outcomes is that the obsession with only goals that are based on outcomes can lead to an "by whatever means necessary" attitude that is extremely risky. It can result in extreme regimens of exercise and diets that help you shed weight fast, yet don't leave you with sustainable practices to sustain, which can make it difficult to sustain outcomes.

A focus on only the outcome will sabotage motivation quite easily. If you only focus on your weight at the bottom of your scale you could get discouraged and forget the possibility of eating the most nutritious diet you've ever had doing regular exercise, and even gaining muscle at first time in a long time!

The most important thing to keep in mind while trying to achieve your goals is this: The world is unpredictable. There will be moments in your life where things happen which can make it more difficult to accomplish your goal. First thing to consider is whether this an incident that is temporary or something that will last longer? If it's a short-term moment, it might be more beneficial to take it easy and move forward at the end of the road, with the progress you've made as long as is possible. If you are experiencing a permanent alteration, then you will need to reevaluate your goals is necessary to ensure you are able to keep moving forward and maintain the drive instead of losing hope.

Making Exercise a Lifestyle

N

You have finally discovered your potential as well as the fact that you're qualified to have an exercise-based and healthy lifestyle and body. So let's examine the benefits of fitness and exercise. This article is intended to help you implement your fitness goals, and not create a specific program specifically for you. If you are looking for more specific information on program design check out our online programs at www.johnwinters.fitness for a customized plan.

The reason I didn't include the exercise program is because exercising is more accurately defined as any type of vigorous or continuous exercise that is performed for long durations frequently. Most people do not like it, or do not have the time to join a gym. Therefore, for the rest of this article in case you don't have a gym among your priorities I would like to encourage you to shake off believing that just exercising in a gym is the best way to stay healthy.

The process of improving your fitness and overall health is simply an issue of getting moving regularly. The majority of people do this by attending the gym. Walking, playing your favorite sports or running around and playing with your children and many more activities can get you started on the path towards better health and wellbeing. It is important to maintain regular physical and mental physical activity as an integral an integral part of living a healthy life because of the positive impact it's been proven to have in preventing the development of chronic diseases.

Comorbidity is the term used to describe that you suffer from more than one illness or disease health condition simultaneously. Some common comorbidities include:

* Diabetes

* Heart disease

* Blood pressure that is high (hypertension)

* High cholesterol

* Obesity

Although advances in medical technology have increased lives, the age when the development of diseases has been similar or, particularly for younger people, is beginning to change dramatically earlier, to the point at which the children of today have a lower life expectancy that their grandparents! Make exercise and physical activity an everyday aspect of your life is one of the most often practiced habits for those older than 60, with a lower number of co-morbidities.

Another benefit of exercising that aids in aging healthfully is to maintain stability, balance and mobility. Falling and tripping is an extremely risky health issue especially for those who are elderly. Regular exercise can help the body to sustain mobility coordination and strength with age. It will enable the body be able to enjoy and do the things you love when you reach retirement and maintain your independence longer getting to and from work safely. Furthermore, increasing research shows that staying physically active can have a beneficial effect on cognitive functioning and also. Increased circulation and improved growth of the red blood cells that is triggered by exercise routine is thought to be the principal cause of this.

When it comes to activities it is when the person is moving, not relaxing, yet is not sufficiently intense to satisfy our expectations for exercise and heart rate increase in addition to increased breathing. sweating. This could mean something as basic that involves standing or sitting or doing a majority of chores that we perform at home.

Incorporating additional activities within your daily routine to enhance the exercise routine is crucial since it will reduce the amount of idle time during your day. The reduction in sedentary hours throughout the day will help shed more calories and fat while keeping your metabolism in check.

This is crucial for those who are in a sedentary position for the majority of their day. Take a break from sitting at your desk with an easy walk through the office or performing some stretching. The more ways you interrupt long hours of sitting for long periods, the more productive.

Take a look at your demands of the day and consider what really requires you to sit at your desk and ways to make you more mobile when you are doing these tasks. Like, walking around during the conference call, or going to speak to one another face-to-face instead of sending an email or even. Be aware that the longer you remain in a stationary position, the less efficient the process gets. It is therefore more difficult to maintain your well-balanced body.

In terms of the kind of exercise that you pick although any exercise is better than nothing even, I'd prefer to are aware of what you can expect from each kind of exercise.

Cardiovascular exercise, or simply cardio, which is what most people are referring to it nowadays can be great for boosting the endurance of your body, while also building better coordination and balance. As the term suggests, it works through enhancing the cardiorespiratory system. This is due to the improvement of lung capacity, function, and delivery of oxygen to blood cells. The quantity of blood cells, and their capacity to absorb oxygen out of the lungs are enhanced, as is the capacity your blood cells are able to retain oxygen, and prepare the heart to perform more effectively flow of blood, as well as the response of your heart after physical effort. Although cardio burns many calories within a brief amount of time, your metabolic body heals and gets in a short time to a normal state.

Strength training is the second main form of training. The strength training process is the one where muscles must overcome a external force. It could be your own the weight of your body or which are free of charge and other machines or items. Similar to the way it sounds it, the primary goal of the training is to improve your endurance. However, the improvements in strength do not only affect your muscles.

Training for strength properly will assist to make the muscles that stabilize stronger as well, but connective muscles and tendons will be prepared to take on external loads more effectively. That's why the majority of physical therapy rehab includes strength-training exercises. The strength training aspect is the place where loading bearing is a factor in order to improve bone density, which can assist in the prevention of osteoporosis.

In addition to increasing strength, keeping and building muscle mass is another major benefit from strengthening. As I said, most of you who read this do not intend to participate at a strength competition or to become the next champion of bodybuilding. It's important to realize that the muscle is one of the primary ways you can direct impact the metabolism of our body. This can be done through two different ways.

One kilogram of muscle can have the average of 50 calories a day in your metabolism at rest. The rate at which this increases or down depends on your preference. Think about the fact that when you reach the age of 25 adults lose about 10 percent in muscle mass each decade. It is mostly due to the lack of activity.

What number of people who are over 40 have heard of complaints that their metabolism is slowing? The metabolism slows down due to decrease. Muscle tissue is a challenge to sustain, and if the body doesn't have any reason for it to stay and eliminate it, then you'll lose it! If clients aren't searching to gain massive amounts of muscle however, I do prepare and inform them that they should anticipate 5-10 pounds of increased muscle mass. The result can increase your metabolism by about 250 to 500 calories per day!

Additionally, the majority of customers who want to slim down want to look the appearance of more muscle and lesser fat. Muscle helps form and shape your body in the way that you'd like to. It is more dense than fat. That means 1 pound of fat takes the most space one kilogram of muscle. Imagine the difference in weight between the bricks of one pound versus one feather pound. When someone loses 10-15 pounds of body fat, while building 5lbs of muscle your scale may display a 10 lb weight difference in weight, yet their physique could be completely distinct.

To lose weight and build the cardio machine is an effective tool as well as strength-training the artist's fine chisels that give us the body we desire.

The other metabolic benefit of resistance training is the afterburn result. If you do your strength workout in the appropriate intensity to you then your body will become much more energetic in the next 24 to 48 days.

The two benefits to metabolism make strength training be an integral part of every weight loss or body weight reduction program. Also, consider the challenges of trying to shed pounds using only an eating plan (or one that focuses on exercise) as much as 50 percent of your weight loss could be due to muscle mass rather than fat. That results in a metabolic rate less than it was when you first started and more frequently, a dislike for the diet that you followed but no desire to follow the same one. Additionally, it will leave your with the lifestyle prior to that while slowly recovering the weight, and a couple of new friends adding to it.

With my clients due to the boost in metabolism the workouts provide and the metabolic boost they receive, they have an energy deficit between 150 and 250 calories due to their routine, with remaining calories are derived from exercise routines as well as afterburn. A client has said "I never pay attention to what I eat during the holidays, but while working with you, this was the first Christmas I didn't put on 20 lbs!" Training for strength properly is only about 20-30 minutes 3-4 times a week, with an ideal time or two between. It will provide a massive return on your time. On other days, it is ideal to fit involved in cardio exercises.

Whatever you decide to engage in, you must be aware of three indicators to consider before you can count the activity as exercise

* Higher heart rate

* A rise in rate and the deep breath

* Perspiration

You need to work out, breath deeply and keep your heart rate up also, and all three are vital. The activity won't be able to cross the line into the realm of exercise until these three have been accomplished for an extended duration regularly.

It is recommended to workout 3-5 times each weekly for 30 to 60 minutes. It is the best way for the improvement of the body's structure, for example keeping a healthy body composition, i.e., fat reduction, improved cholesterol levels as well as lower blood pressure as well as improved blood sugar readings.

If you're not challenging your body, and aren't doing it regularly it doesn't think there is a reason for it to make internal changes to help you conquer the task for you, which is why there's no improvements.

For those who have seen the previous goal to exercise 3 every week for between 30 and 60 minutes, and then freaked out at first, just relax your mind. Like we said, this is the final and best aim of staying healthy. It's not even an initial goal.

The main reason that individuals struggle with incorporating fitness into their lives is due to the fact that they get overly ambitious with the final objective initially. Setting a target which will add one-half to five hours of your daily schedule is a huge mistake to the vast majority. It can cause discontent because of not achieving your goals and a subsequent decrease in the amount of exercise you do until it is to zero. The loss will be the main reason for many people, arguing for failing to try again since it's impossible to get that time back and then you'll just have to repeat the same mistake.

Let's instead try an alternative method. Start small and then gradually moving up towards the final objective is typically more efficient and less time-consuming. It will help you be more successful by reaching small goals and gradually growing your commitment to time and also. Whatever is tiny, is better than nothing in the first place.

In setting your first goals Be realistic about your goals. What you set out to achieve is at the very least one step higher than the work you're currently doing. Keep in mind that even though we might not be able to reach the ultimate target yet, building upon success is much easier than fighting to overcome failings.

If your objective is less than five minutes, do the goal! Sometime, the most challenging part of beginning a fitness program is the fact that you have to start. In the beginning, being ready for exercise but only doing just a little bit is a good step towards the correct direction. Don't be afraid of simply turning up. Dress up, walk outside, visit the gym, or even take your kids to the playground. Being present and making it there is typically the most important thing we can do to get started on doing more. Similar to what we've said about momentum, you'll see yourself taking over five minutes after you've put in the work to make it happen!

When you've decided to start with a little fitness, the next thing to do is to set smaller targets to reach our final goal of 3 every week, for between 30 and 60 minutes. Be aware of every report and posts which go on and on concerning the optimal moment to exercise. If you're not an athlete or the competition you are in is irrelevant. Choose a time and place that works for you, so that you can stay constant and then build up from there.

One of the most simple ways I've found to expanding my exercise time even if you are in the 30-to-60-minute mark is to increase my workout duration by at minimum 1 minute every workout. This solves the problem of having time to make large changes in your time commitment time, and the minute-long increment is more motivating to finish with less doubt about the more you'll need to do to your schedule today.

Similar principles apply to growing the amount of days a week during which you exercise. Begin by adding just one more day. When you are comfortable in your regimen it is possible to add another day when you feel it is necessary.

Let's discuss excuses.

* "I don't have time."

* "I don't have anything to use."

* "I'm too tired."

There are a lot of frequent excuses, but there numerous others. I've worked with individuals across a range of scenarios, and the main distinction between people who experienced the success they did and those who did not is never based on who had a simpler life.

The most important factor in this, and any change in your life lies with the person you. If you're looking to change your lifestyle you must make it your top prioritization and make it a point to figure out a method and follow through. Be aware that exercising is an exercise that boosts your heart rate, speeds up the rate and breath rate, and makes you sweat. This doesn't mean you have you take time away with your loved ones. If having fun with your children will ensure that all three requirements are accomplished for you, take advantage of it. If you're attending a party for children every night, sitting in the evening before the party starts, get out to the park, climb the stairs or, in the case of a sport event, join the group - I promise you the coaches would need support!

If you are a frequent traveler and are not familiar with exercise routines that you can perform at your hotel, take a stroll, or climb the stairs for in a good workout. If you need help putting together a workout for these situations, check out my online coaching tools at www.johnwinters.fitness. Additionally, for traveling some gyms offer access to their facilities with a valid membership. Choose the best price for which location and make sure you sign up.

Sometimes, we get exhausted from our day's working because of the psychological stress that we endure, and not due to physical factors. Our bodies respond to stress the same way - emitting specific hormones to the body. No matter what, your physical life is in danger and you must escape or battle the aggressor, or face deadlines of a major magnitude at work, traffic jams and family obligations at home. Your body reacts in the same manner at a hormonal scale. It's just that when you first encountered the group of stressors physical act was required as an result, whereas in the second it wasn't.

In the event that your body is continuously stressed and has the absence of a physical outlet to restore the hormones released the body can feel fatigued. Also, if the notion of exercising for 30-60 minutes exercising isn't feasible, begin by doing something small. Also, in reference to our discussion on speed, sometimes the smallest adjustments can help get to get you started on your habitual changes. Just getting into your routine of changing into fitness clothes before heading to the gym is an excellent beginning! There is nothing wrong with taking five minutes at first when you're feeling better, take it up a bit at a time.

Always remember that something is superior to nothing. Likewise, it's best to start in a small way and gradually progress through whatever the exercise you choose to do be rather than aiming for the stars and then fail to the point that you lose motivation.

Chapter 4: Overcoming Obstacles

There are some common obstacles to making exercise an habit. On certain days, it may appear as if every force in the universe are conspiring to stop you from doing the gym. In the midst of such a week and it's enough to just give up and abandon the cause. Keep in mind that the entire concept of Consistent Persistence lies in the fact that no matter what obstacles or roadblocks come our way in the long run, as long as you persist with our goal of regular exercise, changes in our lifestyles and our overall health is bound to happen.

Take the lessons learned from your bad days and figure out how you can accomplish the following week to achieve success. Beware of the trap of gimmie-time. When time-related demands unexpectedly are triggered, it's common to see the time we exercise in terms of "gimmie time." I'm sure that you've experienced this, as I've been there. There are so many things piling over that we can look at our exercise time on our calendars and decide, "If I skip my workout, that will give me an extra hour to do this other task." However, the issue is that after doing one time, it's more easy to repeat it. In the end and we're left with none more exercise times, as well as a routine that is not followed. When you are free of the gimmie clock, you can refocus and stay committed to the workout time that you did, and then consider the areas that could be improved.

Many people find this to be as simple as setting new boundaries you set for yourself - i.e. refusing to respond to tasks, when it is the only way you can have the time is to compromise your time for health. It may be challenging to establish boundaries after the people around you have become accustomed to constantly affirming yes. It is possible to need important discussions with family, loved ones, your family members, or even your employer explaining your reasons for concern about your health, you'll take time to care to take care of your body (and fitness) as a top prioritization.

Get them to help in household chores such as chores, bringing kids to school, or any other activity and even making a change the way family time is taken to keep everyone engaged. Sometimes, work-related issues which seem urgent can be handled in the next day or two. It is likely that there will be deadlines to be met, and these will have precedence.

A key part of creating an active lifestyle that makes room to exercise and physical activity is relearning to prioritize tasks at home and work so that you can make space within your daily agenda. It is the reason why starting by building your way up typically more effective than trying to alter your daily routine by adding a two-hour block to be added every week. This often leads to failing because pulling the extra hours from nowhere seems impossible. Begin small, be proud of your accomplishments, then grow upon that.

It could be a matter of adjusting to a different event when our normal one is not accessible, which could comes from changing seasons as well as a shift in our your work schedule or even having children go to different practice or events. Going out on the field as well as helping the team are excellent methods to stay active and support your child's passions.

Sometimes, making the transition from outdoors exercise or activity to something in the house when changes in the seasons is a major factor in many people falling off the routine of regularly exercising. Make a strategy for what your alternative fitness or sport could be depending on the situation so that you can maintain your routine and, most important, to make the most of the time within your timetable. Anything as basic as a simple step that allows you to move up and down an hour or so while you watch the latest show could be an efficient backup strategy when taking a stroll outside can no longer be a viable option.

Keep in mind that the most effective timing for working out is the one that are able to consistently achieve it. What ever the problem the challenge, Consistent Persistence will result in the improvement of our lifestyle and overall health that we want to achieve.

Healthy Nutrition:

A Lifestyle Not A Diet

Examining nutrition plays vital role in maintaining the health of a person because you are the product of what you are eating. Our food choices provide the body with energy together with the necessary nutrients that help to create new cells. Your body will also use the calories and nutrients of our diet to aid in the ability to focus, think and concentrate along with our activity and metabolic rate throughout the day thus, managing weight for either increasing or losing fat, as and maintaining muscles.

Due to this one of the main factors which stands in the way of most of us from better health is the excessive consumption of processed food items. We have all become heavily dependent on these products due to the convenience. However, the processed foods contain a high amount of calories, despite having little or no nutrients they contain, as well as many chemicals the body is not able to use to. Your body is forced to use the few nutrients you take from your food into the process of detoxification, not energy production instead of having the nutrition and energy to provide enough energy to go through the day, and want to be active.

In addition, if your body uses nutrients to detoxification, it could be that you have difficulty maintaining the focus you need or to remain awake while performing mentally difficult activities. They are tempting to consume too much of as our bodies are unable to attain the nutritional balance they require to be content as our body's chemical structure is designed to create cravings.

Do you have any questions about what causes you to be tired despite having enough rest? The reason is that your body does not provide the nutrients required to create energy. Additionally, the majority of processed foods contain sugars that are refined and added to the food. In addition to the calories added to the food you eat, this affects your body's capacity to keep the right weight and body fat level from the metabolic point of view by regulating blood sugar levels and insulin.

Insulin is a natural hormone made by your pancreas, which helps to manage the levels of blood sugar. High blood sugar levels can be detrimental to your body which is why when your blood sugar levels are elevated after doing something such as eating the donut or candy bar the hormone insulin releases for it to return to its normal level.

The body's biochemistry isn't quite up to the technology that permits heavy refining and processing that results in a the highest concentration of sugar into the processed food we consume. It's so simple that it doesn't require much to allow it to be taken from the digestive tract to the bloodstream. It causes rapid and dramatic spikes in blood sugar levels, triggering the release of insulin.

Insulin reduces blood sugar levels since it signalizes your cells to begin storage of the excess sugar. To be stored must transform into fat, which can be stored when your body's metabolism is activated on an excessive regularly, can lead to the accumulation of fat and the weight gain. Because insulin causes your cells to store, the body's capacity to burn off fat decreases a lot regardless of a energy deficit. This is among the main reasons why many suffer from weight loss, even while following their calories recommendations.

To provide you with best quality of nutrition in your diet, stay to the fundamental idea that if someone other than you could not venture outside and look for the item you are looking for, it's most likely that you should not eat it. Make sure you think of as little variation as you can from the field to your the plate. Staying with meats that are natural (not modified) and fruits, veggies and some starches that are as they are in their natural form is the ideal balance for your needs.

Ideally, at every meal the produce portion should comprise the majority of the total volume consumed for the food. It will give you high levels of nutrition and fewer calories. This allows you to be fully satiated and not overindulge in your eating. If you think you require some snacks to go with your meals, these must be primarily based on fruits and vegetables also.

Many people make the error of eating a processed snack which are nutrient-deficient however, they are packed with calories leading us to quickly exceed our calories throughout the entire day. Fruits are an excellent choice for snacks, because they're still simple to take and go, just like some of the snacks, however they provide a higher quantity of fiber and nutrients that will help you stay healthy.

If you're feeling like the fruit you eat isn't enough, then it's likely that you need protein, and instead of more carbs in processed food items. One-serving cheese, about half a cup of nuts or plain yogurt that you serve with fruit are excellent food items that contain protein and are fairly practical. A lot of these snack items can be purchased prepared and packaged into a handy package, in the event that measuring different items takes more time, making this nutritious option feasible.

Apart from the chemically induced cravings triggered by processed food there is a natural tendency to experience cravings for particular taste profiles such as salty, sweet or even savory. It is usually your body seeking specific nutrients that are associated with the particular flavor profile, i.e., sweet fruits that are high in antioxidants. When we opt for foods that have been processed, but with little nutritional value, then you are left with your body still in need of nourishment however, we have consumed more than 200 calories. We may end up feeling hungry but not satisfied because our body requires nutrients, however less calories are available prior to we reach the maximum amount of calories we ought to taking in for weight loss.

If you're searching for something sweet fruit is always a great option, however if you're seeking something more sweet, I suggest researching recipes for fruit compote. Compote made of fruit is made by baking the fruits, which reduces the temperature and increases the sweetness, without adding calories! If you are looking for foods that contain salt like nuts, some cheeses with a moderate amount, or the edamame variety are healthier choices. If you want something savory, proteins is a good choice, as are most meats. Some mushrooms (just be aware regarding the amount of cream that is used in certain recipes) along with some other options for vegetarians are available to help in this kind of desire.

To satisfy cravings for fattier, more rich foods olive oil, certain kinds of hummus or coconut oil fat sources can be a great alternative. If you're using animal fat sources to satisfy your craving for fat take note of the manner in which the animal was raised. Organic or, in the ideal case the free-range, grass-fed variety is ideal since animals that are raised in such a setting are healthier in their fat (cholesterol) levels than those that are traditionally bred. But, take note of the amount of fat sources you consume because fattier food items are more calorie-dense. amount when you're concerned about the weight loss.

Like exercising, this goal is likely to take time to get up to. One way to incorporate an increase in the amount of produce you eat as well as reduce the consumption of processed food items is to focus on each food or snack is consumed in a given day, one at a. As an example, you might begin with dinner, by making it at least 50% of your produce. After your first goal meal is accomplished, then move onto the following.

As you make this change make sure to keep in mind the fact that your protein will only be one quarter of your plate. Likewise, starch should you be able to find it, will take up an entire quarter also. Therefore, even if you're adding some produce chances are you'll have to cut down on the others you've consumed.

When you are taking this new step to improve your fitness and health It is fine to begin with the most delicious foods and snacks. With the number you're working towards the point of being advantageous to begin branching out in order to discover a wider range of flavor options to decrease the possibility of becoming bored with your meals. Additionally, you can try various preparation ways to prepare your meals for a more extensive range of flavors. If you are trying to broaden your options and variety, try a every week a different recipe and preferably with food that you've never had. If you are trying out new food adhere to what I refer to as three rules:

* 3 different cooking methods, i.e., baked, sauteed, grilled

Three different mixes of spices i.e., Italian, southwest, Asian

At least 3 bites from each attempt prior to making a decision about whether or not enjoy it

In the worst case, you've had some thing you did not like this week, but at least it's not possible to declare that you're bored by the food you eat! Most likely, you'll find some new recipes to include in your menu so that you have a greater variety of options for meals when you move forward.

In order to successfully make the change of incorporating more fresh the amount of produce and reducing processed foods to your daily routine, the two main words you need to be aware of is planning and preparation. The primary reason that we see us returning to processed meals in the kitchen or eating at restaurants is that we've not taken the time to ensure that healthy food options are readily available in the comfort of our homes.

Making and planning the meals you will eat is crucial to your overall success. it is often the case that I find the "convenient" meal that I bought out usually took longer than it would have taken to prepare some of my fast, nutritious meal choices when I was properly sure that all the ingredients were available at home.

The initial step is to visit the grocery shop frequently. Because of the increasing amount of food items that is available, it would require a visit at least every week. It's important to ensure that your kitchen fully stocked with what we are supposed to be eating and keep the food that isn't healthy from your home.

It's crucial to ensure that your home is your home a Sanctuary of Health rather than of an Temple of Temptation. It is easy to be enticed in the outside world regardless of whether we are at work, at a party with our friends or at various social events. The knowledge that you are able to make a health and sound choice helps alleviate a lot of anxiety while deciding about your meal choices at other locations.

In preparing your grocery list, you need to think about what you'll prepare for the coming week. This allows you to ensure that you have all the necessary ingredients prior to the time you attempt to repair something. You'll also make sure you don't discover something's not there and ending up at the drive-through.

After you've got all the items that you require for the coming week, it's recommended to begin your meal preparations prior to your meals to be prepared to cook. It is important to wash and cut the fruits and vegetables, to make them easily taken on the move or added when you eat. Cutting and marinating, or seasoning your meat that you'll need can be helpful also. Making these meals in bulk at a time when you can spare the time can help minimize the amount of time spent on the individual preparation of meals, as well as make fruit and veggies more readily available for snacks that are quick and easy to make and snacks. The most efficient way to achieve this is to make cooking part of your shopping schedule, however you are able to plan another time that will meet the needs of your family.

If it's difficult to store your fruits and vegetables for the entire week, you may also make use of frozen products or even store them in your freezer. If you're capable, you can make an additional purchase at the grocery store on a weekday. If so it, then I would suggest making the visit on your way back at the end of your workday, in your gym or anywhere other routes could lead you to a shop on your route. Be aware that this stop is intended to be a short purchase of whatever you need to make it through the remainder of the week. It's not meant to be a shopping all over the store. There is also the option from some of the internet shopping stores that are now open which means all you have to take is grab it at the time you arrive.

If you are forced to dine in a restaurant in order to attend work gatherings with relatives and friends It is likely to be challenging to steer clear of processed food items. Fruits and veggies might or not appear. If you're maintaining your home kitchen well-organized, there is little reason to fret about such incidents so since they're not frequent.

In any dining establishment It is never a bad idea to inquire about alternatives for the volume of vegetables you want as well as you might need reduce the amount of meat to ensure it's in appropriate portions. Ideally, you should have about 3-6 ounces. That's roughly the same size as two decks of playing cards.

If you are hosting a party held at home, with your friends and your family members, you may request to host the party If you're willing. It will give you more control over the food served. If it's going to be a guest house of someone else Ask if it is possible to bring something. It will let you take more food items so that you find what you want and also provide a more healthy more natural, less processed side dish or main meal to provide the option of a healthy and safe choice.

In addition to trying to manage the food options available in social events, one important thing to remember is the importance of portion control. Be careful not to wander around in the area where food is available, since this can result in a subconscious eating habit and over-consumption and not even realizing it. You can eat what you like and then take it to a different place for eating. Be sure to keep track of the amount of plates and high-calorie drinks you've had also.

Most of the time, whether at work or occasions that do not involve food, someone is likely to have something of value to give away. This can be especially true during the holiday season as everyone will have something to offer. Be aware that you're not obligated to consume an equal amount of food even if you don't need that most of the items offered in the first place, or even if you own anything.

Treats and sweets, similar to what we advise our children about drugs, are a thing you should say"NO" to. There are times when we find ourselves food items we never intended to eat because of guilt so as to not offend another person or feeling because of the pressure of others other people having a treat. It's okay to respectfully and say "no thank you. It is acceptable to be able to explain the changes you're making to your way of life. People who will go to make an effort to talk about information with you are likely to support your lifestyle changes you're taking for yourself, too.

The most important thing to keep in mind is that a slip-up or food trap that gets every now and then will not cause you to die. It's okay for unhealthful choices to occur occasionally. But, in order to make sustainable eating habits a part of your lifestyle it is necessary to find the art of balance. I am not a fan of cheat meals or even a day because it imparts too much negativity into the food you choose to eat. But, having food choices that are still enjoyable and are sourced from healthful and less processed foods (and with the right portions) is a way to avoid feelings of feeling depleted that the majority of fast-paced, short-term weight loss plans result in.

It is important to ensure that this isn't becoming an everyday routine each day or week. It is also crucial not to be stressed whenever these situations arise. You will do more harm than good when you try to control something you don't have any control over other instead of just going with your flow and do your best to deal with the circumstance.

In this regard regardless of what we are eating or the reason we eat the food, one thing to pay attention to is the amount of energy that we're placing into the food that we consume. Similar to positive and negative self-talk the energy that is positive or negative that we place into our meals will have profound effects on our health.

Consider your relationship to food. What is the number of times you've consumed food while being a victim of yourself throughout the entire time? It's difficult for our bodies to feel energized and happy when we've slammed ourselves over. When you are able to own it and take pleasure in the experience, you will gain a higher level of energy out of it. It's the same approach when you eat something which is healthy. If you're throwing too much stress on eating it due to the fact that you'd prefer doing something else, it decreases the benefit it could bring you. When you increase your success with healthy food choices you'll have more reason not to be worried over having a bit of enjoyment.

It is recommended to go organic in your food choices whenever is possible. It will get rid of more toxic chemical compounds from your food as well as provide better nutrient assistance from your meals and beverages. Also, purchasing the products of animals free of cages or wild life is the best choice. It is because of the lower exposure to chemicals, and they have higher levels of Omega-3 and Omega-6 fatty acid balance. This helps to lower cholesterol. Animal products are healthier and less contaminated as compared to conventional foods because they're less likely to be a source of bacteria that are resistant to acid that cause acid resistance, such as E. coli.

A common omission in nutritious nutrition is adequate hydration. The recommended minimum amount of fluid is 64 ounces per day that's about eight cups, or two Liters. Be aware that 64 oz is the bare minimal amount. A common recommendation is to calculate the weight of your body in pounds and divide it in half. This number represents the amount of ounces you have to consume. If, for instance, you weigh 150 pounds the half weight of that is 75. Therefore, the daily amount of water you drink is 75 ounces.

I've noticed that a lot of individuals don't reach this point with different fluids they consume. Being dehydrated puts extra pressure on the body because it's having a difficult time clearing toxins as well as maintaining electrolyte balances. Although it may sound contradictory and yet the more fluids you consume in a day, the more water the body retains trying to keep the balance of its fluids. If you drink adequate water on a regular schedule, your body has no reason to retain it because of the consistent intake.

Furthermore water is a crucial element in the procedure of burning fat. Thus, running from every day with no water could limit your fat burning capacity. If you're trying to lose your weight (again water is required for fat burning, however, it is also essential for building muscle) increase your intake by 8-16 oz each day. When you exercise, make sure to you should add an additional 8-16 oz, and when you are outside, add another 8 ounces for every hour outside - possibly more based on humidity and temperature.

I would like to make clear that this recommendation should be for only water. Drinking alcohol that is with a high sugar content or diet drinks that contain harmful chemicals are not helping to hydrate because they're water-based liquids already in solution.

The body makes use of water to maintain the dissolved substances the body needs naturally and creates, like minerals and vitamins, as well as waste substances in the right levels. A majority of these fluid sources can create acidity and put your body in the balance. The body requires additional fluids in order to flush out the undesirable chemicals in the majority of refined drinks. Additionally, if we drink beverages that have calories added in conjunction with meals however, they do not affect our bodies satiety which is the feeling of being fuller and makes the beverage calories additional when it comes down to fighting hunger.

If you are able to drink juices, be sure that they're truly pure juices and must be consumed in smaller portions. It is best that they are fresh squeezed, and certainly not concentrated or have excessive amounts of sugar added.

If you are able to consume the juices with no food, it must be consumed slowly over a lengthy duration, as unlike eating a whole fruit as a snack the juices contain very little of the fiber that which you could have gained when eating the whole fruit. Although a cup of juice might contain nearly exactly the same calories, without fiber, juices may trigger a spike in sugar and trigger an undesirable hormone called insulin. When you drink the juice more slowly, it can spread out the response to blood sugar, which lowers the need for insulin.

If you are looking to lower the amount of sugar you consume and primarily want flavour, instead of drinking regular drinking water, mixing in a little amount of juice in water is a great way to help, without putting in a large calories. Try using the slices of fruit or some sea salt, or Himalayan pink salt to aid in flavor as well as water usage.

Increase your water intake is an exercise to be done slowly in order in order to give your body a opportunity to adapt. I would suggest adding by 8 ounces or less the daily total. Do this for at least 2 to 3 weeks. If you're still not reaching the 64-ounce mark, you can raise it by similar amounts and continue each week for a couple of weeks until you've achieved your desired amount of ounces. As you gradually increase your intake of water and your body will be more able to adapt to it more easily and will experience lesser issues in excess bathroom usage. Keep your mind in the present that you must frequent the bathroom on a regular basis to enable the body to flush out any toxins.

For 64 ounces daily water consumption it is likely that you have a container at hand to drink water throughout all whole day. This is simpler than trying to smash down several glasses of water every time you are close to a source of water.

Additionally, if the source is within reach, then there's a chance that you'll become more aware of this than when it's inside the fridge or in the sink you are only able to see at a couple of times a the day.

It is a good idea to avoid placing any plastic bottles inside the vehicle. The result is often unneeded chemicals leaking in the water. Additionally, it may result in it becoming too hot during heat of summer for you to desire to drink more which defeats the goal. If you would like the cooler temperature of your water I would suggest making use of ice, or freezing a portion of the water that is in your bottle, or an insulated bottle that you can reuse.

Chapter 5: Sleep to Your Health

Another vital element of good health which is frequently neglected is sleeping. Few of us can get the required 7-9 hours of rest every evening. The reason for this is that it is during this time that your body gets the highest amount of regenerating cells. When the process ceases and your body begins your day in a state of tension, no matter how easy or challenging your work schedule. You can see, beginning your day physiologically in a state of stress is likely for a continual accumulation of stress for the remainder of the day. This can result in becoming less capable of handling any stressors that may arise.

The most basic ways to get better rest include not drinking coffee, getting some light exposure throughout the day and staying away from screen-based activities for the first hour of going to the time you go to bed. These include computer screens, TVs, or even mobile phones. By doing this, you can help ensure that your sleep patterns are at a more optimal level for bedtime.

Certain things can be helpful to improve your psychological state. Beware of doing activities that cause wakefulness during your sleep. If you can train your mind and body to remain awake even when sleeping in the daytime, you will be able to remember that during the night, even if attempt to rest.

Making a bedtime routine is also beneficial. Many of us follow schedules that we follow to prepare to go to work, after we have returned home, as well as other tasks that we carry out throughout the morning. They help prepare your body and mind to anticipate the future and the expectations of you. Many people believe to simply get off their task to fall into bed and instantly go to go to sleep. Or, when they have fallen asleep for some time in their living space, they will be in a position to rise and get back to sleep with no impact on your sleep. This is not a realistic belief.

Establishing a routine for bedtime helps you unwind and prepare for sleep. It can be as brief or long as you believe that it is necessary however the most important thing is to ensure that you're doing exactly the same thing, with the same sequence like:

* Brushing your teeth

* facial wash, or another products for skin care

* bathroom

* stretches

* reading, preferring to do it with print, not screen time

* light out, eyes shut to sleep

What you decide to include on your schedule is completely the decision of your own. You can make it as complex or as simple as you like however, if you follow it regularly it will aid the body and mind connect this routine to sleeping. The routines mentioned above could be extremely helpful to people with a variety of work hours and people who frequently travel to job.

A different issue that can affect sleeping is stress. It usually comes in the form of issues we're worried about that hinder our ability to fall asleep or issues that could cause us to wake up during the night and we do not wish to remember. Journals can aid in either of these reasons.

If you are immersed in a trance of the day as you lay in bed, trying to get sleep Write down all the thoughts you've got in your mind. No matter the format you choose to use, be it a list, venting or even reminiscing about your entire day. The goal is to take all your thoughts out and clear your head by writing everything into your journal. It is also possible to make use of a journal to record those thoughts that come into your thoughts and that you do not wish to lose. Keep a journal using and keep it near the bed. Then, whenever it occurs, you can note it down. So, it will be ready for you to look over each morning, once you're well-rested to take a good look and tackle the issue.

If your issue is merely not allowing enough time to sleep the same way as the other objectives, you should begin by adding more time to your sleeping slowly. It is possible to do this by extending your sleep time into the morning hours, or adding just a bit of both the evening and in the morning or simply time during the night. The best time individuals can add to their evenings is at night, because many of us are taking our daily time in the morning to its limit. When you can add a tiny amount of time every week, it is easy to modify your evening schedule in order to accommodate the shift.

It is recommended to first identify non-essential viewers from your evening. Most of us is watching television. It is recommended to invest for a streaming or recording device if the shows you love is something you're unwilling to give up. It will give you more freedom and control over your timetable.

Similar things that are not contributing to your health should be evaluated. Check how much time spend on them to determine what you can do to find a compromise that will allow you to get the ability to rest and continue doing the things you enjoy. Anything that makes you fighting with your mindless eating habits are an excellent place to begin. You will have the time to rest and less stress from eating late into the night. It is also an excellent method make time for workout and meal preparation.

A second thing to be mindful of is the practice of avoiding revenge. The reason for this is that we deliberately delay getting ready for bed in retaliation for the long, hard or tiring day of work which allowed the least amount of relaxation. This can be a very dangerous trap If not taken care of, it will result in endless hours of sleeping each evening. Set aside time for leisure every night, but adhere to your time limit. If you've only got the one or two episodes to be watched and you're not satisfied with what shocking ending the ending was keep watching!

After we've discussed diet, hydration, and sleeping, I'd want to discuss these topics and how they impact the threshold for stress. Similar to your stamina, endurance and endurance, our bodies have limits on the amount of stress we are able to take on before we are ready to let go. If you've never experienced it, you've probably witnessed it. It's a simple thing that happens suddenly, and abruptly it's a complete breakdown. It doesn't matter if it's crying or anger it's impossible to smother the exploding feelings we've tried to keep under control. Whatever it is, physical or mental and it all adds up increasing and testing the boundaries of our tolerance to stress.

Sleeping in and being tired as well as dehydration and malnutrition are all triggers. When you awake following a long night of poor sleep, dehydrated due to having not gotten enough fluids prior to the day and deficient in the amounts of nutrition to sustain the body's health and function beginning your day with three significant stressors that are stacked against this threshold. This reduces the amount of stressors that you are able to manage throughout the duration of your day. A good night's rest, proper food, and water intake is a great way to improve not just your overall health but also how hard the task may appear.

Lifestyle Changes and Family

Many of you might be thinking"oh, I'm sorry, "Wow! That would be very effortless if I did not have to convince my family members involved." The first thing to note is that it's true. It's generally easier when they involve little or no influence on anyone else. But, none of the suggestions in this article are advised to the majority of people. Only those who be more prone to difficulties are people who have disabilities or suffer from severe food restrictions because of health issues. The majority of people believe that the modifications discussed in this publication are helpful to everyone.

What is essential for making an alteration in lifestyle of a family unit is to communicate. If everyone else isn't informed of the changes that you're trying to implement or the reason behind taking them on, you'll be faced with a variety of obstacles and temptations that can lead to a snare - with no guidance or accountability to aid you succeed when issues occur. However If everyone knows of the healthier lifestyle changes you're trying to achieve, it'll make it easier to get assistance with food purchases and cooking along with time for exercise.

The most frequent problems I've heard people talk about are their children. It doesn't matter if it's getting time to fitness or making changes to your diet People often cite their children as the main motivation for them to not try or giving up healthy choices in their lives.

As we've mentioned before, children do not need to be separate from you to allow you to get exercise. It is possible to do activities with them, like cycling, walking, or any other game in the event that you experience the higher heart rate, increasing speed and breathing, as well as sweating throughout the exercise. If your children are in many different programs that they're involved with take a stroll prior to the event. If it's an activity for sports, figure out ways to support players during training so that you are in motion. Maintaining a healthy lifestyle particularly with your kids engaged, creates a positive example for them to look up to for inspiration in the future.

In the case of changing your diet and feeding your children's nutrition, I'm going to make one point before we can move on. Kids Don't Need Junk Food! Parents make the claim that they keep things in their homes since their children "need" it. It's been a while since I've found an authoritative source which states that it's acceptable for children to indulge in things such as chips, candy or fast food and desserts. regularly.

Try to adhere to your plan to limit the consumption of processed food can be a challenge if you allow your home to turn into an Temple of Temptation instead of an Sanctuary of Health, just because you keep things in the kitchen for your children. Treat foods should no longer be considered treat if they're the norm of a person's diet. Like the rest of us, treat foods ought to be treated as a few times a year for children.

The habits we establish for eating in our childhoods frequently set the foundation for the choices we make in our nutrition choices when we are adults. If you wish for your children to become well-rounded adults, teach your children the skills to be successful from an early age. Like I said earlier in this guide, you must always keep an effort to be healthy while talking with and helping your children make making these lifestyle changes. Allow them to help decide of goals you'd like them to select for the year, be it what you'll do to stay active or exercising together as a family, or what vegetables you'd like in your food, or having them decide on new dishes to test. As you increase their participation in making decisions of goals, the greater trust and commitment they'll get for you in the future.

The process of making these changes when the family is familiar with a healthier way of life is likely to take time. In dealing with children and taking nutritional adjustments (and change in activity) it is important to always be on feeling healthy and healthier. Parents should be warned against talking about diets as well as weight loss and another negative self-talk that focuses on the way we appear and perceive ourselves.

When I see clients who come with their families, we do not talk about getting rid of fat and weight, with the exception of the most severe of situations. The children notice our motives as well as our reasons for making changes, and will always be paying attention. Make sure that you emphasize that the changes you're doing are for your personal benefit, to your own health and wellbeing, which means you're able to participate in more vigorous activities together. Never do you think thinking that you're losing weight on account or because of the opinion of other people or to appear better or look more appealing. This is all about staying fit and healthy.

Also, establishing a proper program for modeling our children will benefit the kids and for us. When you are working towards making your family more active as well as nutrition, it's appropriate to take a step-bystep strategy as previously discussed in the other areas. The most important thing is to ensure that everyone is on the same page with each small step in order in order to reach the ultimate goal. It's usually beneficial to let other members of your family know which next action to take. This will help to gain more involvement and support by everyone who is in the process.

A key aspect to consider when goals is to let the world know about the goals you have set. One of the biggest mistakes that many people make is limiting our objectives in our own minds. If you're the only one to know that you're eating a healthy diet and stay fit, you are likely to face many more choices, since no one else has the knowledge that you are not being lured by them. Additionally, it is more easy to succumb to temptations since you're the only person responsible for your actions and there is no one else to help you.

It is often done so that we can avoid issues such as guilt, or embarrassment of not being able to fulfill the promises which we've said we would. The only person you'll who is truly disappointed when you let go of the goal you set is yourself. But, those who inform their loved ones and family members be aware of their plans generally have higher chances of accomplishment. Although, certainly, a part of it can be due to the fact that you avoid shame or guilt for not achieving your goals, another aspect is the help you will need it during times of desire.

If you're letting individuals around you be aware of the goals you have set and seeking their help and support, you must engage them in a discussion regarding what you would like the support they provide to be. A common reason why people do not reveal to their loved ones and family members be aware of their plans is due to the fact that their "support" they end up receiving can prove to be more annoying and irritating than it is actually useful. Most of the time, this is because of the lack of family members and friends understanding the meaning behind the word "support. Therefore, be 100% clear about what you would like and wouldn't need from everyone before you start your search.

I've observed that through my experience dealing with clients, some actually want that non-mercy drill sergeant, who shows no regret in doing the do their job and make their accountable to the actions they are doing independently - in terms of fitness and nutrition monitoring. Some prefer caring and compassionate support to help them determine the best course of action in case they fall and take note of what's holding their back. Consider what that you really want from your family members and close friends in terms of support in general, as well as the support you require individually from your closest friends and family members.

Another way of assistance is to have someone who has made changes along together with you. This will allow you to get the support of someone who is facing similar struggles to you as well as someone to assist in brainstorming ways to conquer these obstacles. In the case of close friends and family there is the majority of your changes will be made by other people regardless of the modifications that you make. One of the toughest difficulties I encounter in my job of helping others is understanding:

To allow healing to happen patients must accept the possibility of healing.

The best thing you can accomplish is to keep making positive lifestyle changes and be an example to those close to you, while also letting them know that you're here to assist them when they're prepared.

Make sure that their resistance to change does not affect your decisions to remain fit and healthy. There are times when it is important to pick your choices.

If you're aware of certain foods that won't be healthful with these foods, then any meals that you can eat without them must be on the right track! If you are aware of days that will not be a good time to incorporate an exercise routine, don't count to include those days in your think about it and plan on it in order to achieve success.

Chapter 6: Understanding the power of "consistency"

The power of consistency is not just limited to the activities we do in our day to day life. It can also be applied to many other aspects of our lives.

Consistency is a very important and powerful trait that we should try and cultivate in all aspects of our lives, as it has the power to transform us into better human beings. Consistency is what makes us who we are today.

The power of consistency has been proven over time and it's only natural that we too understand its importance and practice it as much as possible.

One of the most powerful things that we can do in life is to be consistent. Consistency is the secret for success.

We look at consistency as a vital requirement for any kind of progress in life. We might not know the exact reason why it has such a powerful effect but it does. Some people say that consistency is all about making sure that your actions speak louder than your words, which means you should be consistent in everything you do so that your actions are what other people will remember you by.

When we are consistent in what we do, it gives us the feeling of being in control of our lives. It allows us to see progress or growth when we learn something new.

There are many benefits of being consistent in anything in life, but one is that it allows us to have an idea on what our limits are and how much effort we put into anything that takes place in our lives.

The truth though, is that there is no such thing as 'perfect consistency', but we need to understand the power of consistency in whatever we do in life.

Consistency is one of the most important traits that can make or break a person. If we want to be successful and compete at the top, we need to start practicing and develop our consistency skills. It doesn't matter what area of life we are talking about, it's all about being consistent.

This chapter will help you understand how important consistency can be in any aspect of your life and how it can affect your future success.

There are many successful examples of people who have achieved their goals by maintaining consistency. Albert Einstein put it this way, "I cannot imagine a person who leads a life without putting in some thought about the meaning of it."

Some people find consistency to be boring and they often give up because they think that they are not making progress fast enough. However, the benefits of consistency may not be seen straightaway but can be felt much later on.

As we read continue reading through this chapter, we will find out how consistency in life can lead to success in any endeavor or goal. It goes on to say that it is not just reflected in our careers but also in our hobbies and personal relationships. It explains that consistency can produce results even when we are faced with difficulties.

Understanding the power of consistency in whatever we do in life is important, and the key to success.

There are many successful people who have achieved their lives' dreams because they knew how to be consistent. They applied this principle and got what they wanted in life by making it happen each and every day.

If you think about it, consistency is everywhere. It can be seen in the way we dress, the way we eat, and even the way we go to work. It can be seen in everything that we do.

That's why it's so important for us to know how to use it properly in our lives; because if we don't, then our lives will just get messy and complicated. That's why I want you to think about: how consistency can help your personal life and your professional life.

We can increase the probability of success if we are consistent with whatever we do. We should try to be the same person in all our surroundings and interactions.

The power of consistency is not just in how it helps us to be more successful, but also in how it affects the people around us. People subconsciously associate certain actions with certain traits, so if you are always consistent, people will think that you are reliable, loyal and dependable.

It is the ability to do something day in and day out without any interruption. This can be done in many aspects of life, such as school, work, fitness, relationships and more. When done correctly, consistency can turn into a habit.

It's because consistency is what helps us establish habits. For example, if we eat healthy every day for breakfast or do 10 push-ups every morning for 3 weeks straight before work then it becomes habit for us to continue it even after those 3 weeks are over.

In the book, "The Power of Habit", author Charles Duhigg discusses the power of habit and how it affects our lives. The good news is that there is a lot we can do to change what habits we have or to create new habits. These changes will lead to a more productive and happier life.

What does this have to do with consistency?

Everything! Understanding consistency is key to changing our habits and creating new ones because consistency is the small things that we do every day that lead us into huge transformations over time.

It is important to understand the power of consistency because it is important for success. It is not only a key factor in carrying out our dreams, but it also improves them and helps us achieve them.

One example is when we want to build a better future for ourselves and others. When we are consistent in our actions, we can make a powerful impact on this world that lasts forever.

In his book, Eric G. Bradlow teaches us to understand the power of consistency in whatever we do in life. He makes a compelling case for why consistency is important and how it can make a big impact on our lives.

What he also advocates for is that we should be consistent with everything to create a positive chain reaction that will lead to success or failure.

He also tells us that when we take time to be consistent, it will not only help ourselves but also those around us who might need the support and reassurance from someone who has been there

The power of consistency is undeniable. It doesn't matter if it's in our physical appearance, our personal habits, or just the way we keep things organized. Consistency plays a role in everything that we do.

So what happens when we apply this power to writing?

Writing in a consistent manner gives you the ability to grow and succeed in your writing career. It can help you build and maintain your reputation by staying true to your style and voice across all of the different mediums that you use to represent yourself professionally.

It can also help you become better at what you do by training your brain and enhancing your work ethic over time.

This is because when we write consistently; it becomes easier for us to focus on writing because we know exactly what we need to do each time -

Understanding the power of consistency is a life-changing lesson. It is one that will help us to live a more fulfilled and happy life. It is a lesson that will teach us to enjoy the little things in life more.

It does not matter if we are talking about our careers, relationships, or hobbies – consistency really does have a powerful impact on our lives.

"It is possible to achieve anything in life with consistency. Success is not about getting lucky, it's about doing the right things day in and day out."

-Ryan Holiday

Consistency can be achieved by implementing some of these habits into our daily routine:

- Structure your morning routine, do the same thing every single morning to get your day started.

- Prioritize your time by focusing on one task at a time.

- Take care of the important tasks first, they are usually more difficult than the simpler tasks.

- Keep track of your progress on a daily basis.

It doesn't matter if you are trying to build a business, lose weight or achieve any other goal. Achieving the goal only becomes possible if you are consistent with it. This article will help you understand how consistency can help lead you to success in life and business in such a way that will make your life easier and more productive.

What can we do when we feel like quitting?

We all experience difficult times at some point in our lives and it takes courage and resilience to become creative in finding the solutions for these problems.

A lot of people say that consistency is the key to success in life. They are not wrong. Consistency is an important aspect of life that has the power to change our lives for the better. This section will help us understand the power of consistency and how it can be used for better living.

A lot of people think that they need to have all the skills in order to be successful in their fields. But this is not true, what they actually need is consistency. Which means following through on their promises or goals, day after day, week after week, month after month etc., no matter what gets thrown at them.

By being consistent in everything one does in life, one can start seeing changes happen quickly and efficiently and so, quitting will never be an option.

In everything that we do, consistency matters a lot. It is the only way that we can develop habits and form better versions of ourselves. Life is a journey and by following this idea of consistency, we can see more progress and success in all aspects of our life.

The power of consistency is the one thing that holds us back from achieving our goals. However, it also helps us grow exponentially.

It's easy to think of the power of consistency as something we need to learn and do in order to achieve our goals and grow as a person. But let's turn this around and think about the power of consistency as a barrier for us - not a tool we use to achieve our goals.

This is because we naturally want to shift things up and try new things, which gets you out of your routine and creates opportunities for failure.

Consistency and how important it is in our lives as marketers.

With today's changing times, we often feel like any success we achieve is short-lived. We spend most of our time feeling like an impostor, always on the verge of being found out as a fraud.

However, there is one trait that has been proven to hold across all fields and all industries: consistency. Consistency gives us something solid to rely on when everything else seems uncertain.

It allows us to start building up a sense of self-efficacy so that we can face other obstacles with greater ease. Most importantly, consistency helps us remember who we are even when the outside world tries to tell us otherwise.

Consistency is critical for success. It is important to find a balance between consistency and variety. Some people find it easier to stick with what they know and others need the constant shift in order to stay focused and motivated.

All successful people use some form of consistency. And it doesn't matter what type of person you are, you should always be aware of the power that consistency has in our lives.

Understanding the power of consistency is an important first step towards taking control of our lives.

Consistency is one of the most powerful tools we have as human beings. It's so powerful, it can even change our lives and shape our destiny. If you want to be more successful, healthy, and happy, consistency is your best friend.

Life is a series of events that are interconnected. These events, both good and bad, are what make us who we are. But if things weren't consistent in our lives, these events would have little to no meaning or relevance to us.

People often underestimate the power of consistency. It is one of the most powerful ways to attract and retain customers.

Consistency is an important part of any business strategy and it enables you to achieve your goals and this will be discoursed in details when we get to chapter three. The power of consistency means that if you have a clear direction for your business, then you will be able to turn your vision into reality.

It also means that if you have a specific goal in mind, then the best way to reach it is by following a specific strategy with consistency.

There are many benefits to consistency. It brings stability, reassurance and familiarity to our lives. It helps us achieve goals and reach our full potential. It also reduces stress and increases happiness and self-confidence.

You might think that consistency is boring, or that it won't make you happy. But the truth is, consistency is the key to happiness. We all need a sense of stability and routine in our lives; it's what makes us feel content. If you want to be happy, then you need to make sure your life stays consistent.

Everyone wants their lives to be different and better than they are now, but the power of consistency is what we should all be striving for. Whether it's in your health, relationships or career, consistency is key and will get you much further than sporadic bursts of energy.

Consistency is a common theme that you hear from successful people – they make a plan and stick with it. Successful people know that life can be full of unpredictability, but they also know that there are ways to make the unpredictable more predictable by setting goals and sticking to them.

This basically means we should be consistent in our daily actions and behaviors. We should strive to do the same set of tasks each day, whether it's going to the gym, spending time with family or meeting deadlines at work. The more we can find consistency in our lives, the happier and more successful we will feel.

Chapter 7: Consistency against all odds

In this chapter, I took my time to highlight the importance of being consistent in whatever we do in life against all odds and then offer a few tips to help us be consistent.

People who are consistent in life generally against all odds are more likely to be successful than those who are not consistent. There are many benefits that come with being consistent - one's work will be successful and they will have healthier relationships with people around them.

People want to follow someone who has the same values every time they interact with them; this way other people can trust that person and know what they will get if they spend time with them.

We see people who have been on the same diet for years and they look healthy and fit. We also see people who have been on the same exercise plan for years and they look really good. These people are consistent with their actions, despite all odds.

The first thing that comes up in our mind when we hear about consistency is "being stubborn" or being persistent without any hope of success. I don't think this negative connotation fits these people as well as it fits others because these people are consistently doing something without any hope of success.

What do you think?

Being consistent in whatever we do in life against all odds is a valuable character trait for us to have. It is the key to success and every success story has consistency as a factor. In this chapter, I will tell you about an example of a successful business man who lived his life by being consistent and what he did to be successful in that endeavor.

I will cover some qualities that the man possessed which had a big effect on his success and also some qualities which he lacked but caused him to fail despite all of the hard work that he put into it.

I hope that through these examples, I can inspire you to be more consistent in whatever you do in your life no matter how difficult the circumstances might be.

Being consistent in whatever we do in life against all odds, is the key to success. It does not matter what you do or who you are, but it's important to be consistent with your decisions and actions..

It is not an easy task to be consistent in what we do in life. We all face ups and downs which can lead us to doubt our decisions and think about quitting. But it is important to keep on going no matter how hard it gets. This is because there are many cases where people have achieved what they wanted just by being persistent.

Some of the benefits of consistency are that we build up our willpower, improve our self-confidence, acquire new skills, set good habits, and gain valuable experience which will help us in the future.

There are a number of reasons why we should be consistent in whatever we do in life. One of the main reasons is the uncertainty of life. If we are not consistent, we will never know what will happen to us when it comes to our finances, relationships and careers.

Another reason is that consistency gives us a sense of control over our lives. This feeling may be false because there are many things that happen in life that are outside our control but it is still better if we have some sense of certainty about them at least.

We may not see the results as we wish to, but we need to keep going and trust that the things will work out for us.

What we must do is to find what we want to be consistent in. Then we should identify the consequences, benefits and obstacles. Next step is identifying our motivation and finally take action.

I have always been a consistent person. You can see that in my academics, professional life, and personal life. When I was in school, I would study for hours on end to get the best grades possible. When I entered college,

I took on part-time jobs so that I could focus more on my studies. This consistency has carried over to not only what goes on in my head but also how I present myself to the world around me.

The reason why consistency is so important is because it helps you build trust with other people and lets you know where you stand at all times.

It also keeps your self-confidence high because it means that no matter what happens in life, there will be someone who will be there for you and understand your journey.

It is tough to do what we want all the time. We're constantly being pulled in different directions, and it can seem hard to say no to anything. We should be careful, though. There are consequences for not being consistent in what we do in life against all odds.

We can give up on our goals. We might be less productive at work and fail to achieve what we set out for ourselves. And most importantly, it will make us unhappy with ourselves because of this lack of consistency.

In life, we are always faced with a dilemma of either being consistent or taking the easy way out. The former leads to a fulfilling career and the latter leads to a life full of regrets.

Do not be afraid to take risks when the opportunity arises. Be persistent in your pursuits and don't give up after one failure. Lastly, never let anyone tell you who you should be or how you should live your life.

It is important to be consistent in whatever we do in life against all odds. We need consistency not only in our work but also outside the workplace. It is essential to stick with our goals, see them through to the end, and never give up even if the going gets tough.

The success of a person is not just about how they work and what kind of work they do. It's also about their consistency and how they always keep up to their standards.

The most important thing we should learn from the life stories of these successful people is that consistent effort can change your life no matter what you are doing.

People often stop because they feel like what they are doing is not enough or it's too hard for them to stick with it, but in reality it's just that their thoughts are stopping them from being consistent in the long term.

We can use consistency as a way to hold on to our sense of self. We may not be able to keep up with all of the changes in society, but we can still find consensus within ourselves.

People often say, "Those who can't do teach." But those who do teach often find it difficult to stick to a regimented schedule and stick with what they preach. Part of the issue is that we like to indulge in our weaknesses rather than our strengths.

The need for consistency is becoming more and more important for people, as we go through life we need to be able to rely on ourselves and know that we will follow through with what we want no matter how hard it may be.

Many people think that consistency in life is not possible and they think they will not be able to be consistent with their work.

We see people put in a lot of hard work and then give up when they experience failures. Consistency in life is about staying focused on your goal and never giving up.

Consistency is more important than ever. We all have the responsibility to make the world a better place for future generations.

It doesn't matter if you are a mother, father, daughter, son, sister, brother or any other family member. The time has come to break down those barriers and be as consistent as possible in what we do in life against all odds.

It is not always easy to stay the course. We are constantly faced with conflicting priorities, changing priorities, and competing demands.

Sometimes you will find yourself doing things that are not in alignment with your goals. This is where consistency becomes the key. As the wise saying goes "If you don't stand for something, you'll fall for anything".

We should always try to be consistent in whatever we do in life. This will make us less likely to make mistakes. It will also help us achieve our desired outcome. No matter how difficult the situation is, you should never give up.

This is the hardest part of it, consistency against all odds. But it is also the most important one because it is what makes everything else possible.

It is not easy to be consistent in life. Most of the times, we are faced with challenges that make it hard for us to stay on track. There are times when we feel like quitting and giving up because of all the obstacles that come our way. However, there are ways that help us stay consistent in what we do in life even when things get tough.

1) Be Present: Being present is the most important factor in staying consistent. Whatever you do or whatever happens to you, being present makes you think more clearly and helps you focus on your tasks at hand.

2) Create a Support System: In order to stay consistent, it is important to have a support system which consists of people who understand what you're going through and will be there for you no matter what

The true secret to living a life that is consistent, then, is to find what makes you happy and do that. It's not about achieving anything in particular; it's about enjoying where you are.

The secret to living a life that is consistent is about finding what makes you happy and doing that. You don't need to achieve anything in particular; it's about enjoying where you are.

Everyone has their own idea of what makes them happy, but often times just taking time for yourself can help create that consistency.

The truest measure of success is how much you enjoy your life. The true secret to living a life that is consistent and fulfilling, then, is to find what makes you happy and do that. It's not about achieving anything in particular; it's about enjoying where you are.

With a little time and effort, consistency can become a habit against all odds.

I believe that by now, we all know that consistency is the key to success. It's what separates the best from the rest, but it can be hard to achieve. There are many obstacles that get in the way like lack of time, lack of motivation and even social pressure. But with a little time and effort, consistency can become a habit against all odds.

It's not always easy to maintain consistency. How many times have you said you would go to the gym and then gone for a long walk instead? Or promised yourself you would be more compassionate and then lashed out at your loved one?

Consistency is one of the most powerful forces in human psychology. It's what leads to success in all areas of life, from dieting to financial planning.

The human mind is a powerful and mysterious thing. It can lead us to do both amazing and terrible things, and it can't always be controlled.

 The natural impulse of the mind is to want to go with the flow, but this can sometimes lead to complacency. The more we practice something, though, the more likely it will become a habit.

Most people, when asked what they want to accomplish in a day, will list a few things. But the truth is that these things will only lead to disappointment if they are not properly prioritized.

When someone sets out to do something for them, it should be done with the understanding that it will take some time and effort before it becomes a habit against all odds.

As life speeds up, many people find themselves struggling to keep up with their daily routines. But there are ways that you can create a routine that ends up being enjoyable, rather than a chore.

As life speeds up, many people find themselves struggling to keep up with their daily routines. But there are ways that you can create a routine that ends up being enjoyable, rather than a chore.

Many people find themselves struggling to keep up with their daily routines, but there are ways that you can create a routine that ends up being enjoyable, rather than a chore.

Yes, we all know already that one of the toughest things to do in life is maintain consistency. There are so many distractions and disruptions that can pull you away from your goals, but with a little time and effort, consistency can become a habit against all odds.

One of the most difficult things to do is develop healthy habits. This is especially true when it comes to self-care. However, if you can take small steps and make them a part of your life, they eventually become second nature. The key to this is to know where to start and what the benefits are.

Achieving consistency is no easy task, but with a little time and effort, it can become a habit against all odds.

When it comes to social media, how often have you noticed that after a while, all of your social media posts are sounding the same? It can't be avoided. But don't worry; it's not your fault. It's hard to maintain consistency in writing when you're multitasking and juggling different projects.

Keeping up with an active social media feed is tough, but with practice and some helpful tips, it can become second nature for

Consistency can be difficult to keep up with everything--especially with all the distractions that come with modern life. Despite this, it is important for people to exercise consistency in order to reap its benefits.

It can be difficult to uphold in any aspect of life, but once it becomes a habit, it's easier to keep up with. By identifying the areas where consistency is lacking, one can focus on those aspects and slowly build up consistency over time.

Habits are tricky, but if you set goals for yourself, it can be easier to be consistent.

The more goals you set for yourself, the more likely you are to stick to them. For example, if your goal is to maintain a healthy lifestyle and exercise regularly, you could also make goals like updating your fitness app every time you workout, or buying healthier foods.

One of the most difficult things about forming habits is that we often feel like we just can't be consistent. However, if you set goals for yourself and then use a system to track your progress, it's easier to stay on track and do what you're supposed to do.

Setting goals is a great way to be more consistent. If you want to run every day, set a goal of running 5 days per week. If you want to read more books, set a goal for yourself of reading 1 book per month. Not only will achieving your goals make you feel good about yourself, it will help you become better at the skill or habit that you are working on.

Habits can be hard to establish, but they will make your life easier if you set goals for yourself. Consider your habits as a ladder- climbing up to the next rung can be tough, but you need to make sure you have a goal in mind before you start the climb. If your goal is fitness related, then break it up into smaller steps and set manageable goals that will produce results over

However, forming a habit is more likely if you set goals for yourself and the steps you need to take to achieve those goals. So, for example, if your goal is to work out three times a week, you should plan your workouts at the same time every day and try not eat anything right before or after those workouts

Do you have the same routine every morning? How about your evening routine?

I usually wake up every morning and take a glass of water, and then have my shower, and then I go to the kitchen and have breakfast. After breakfast, I'll do some dishes and laundry before getting ready for work.

At work, I'll answer emails, attend meetings, or work on a project. When I get home from work, I'll do some more laundry and cook dinner before watching TV with my family until bedtime.

A morning routine can be anything from reading over your calendar, checking the weather forecast, to making a cup of coffee. The way that you choose to start your day is up to you.

You can also create your own evening routine based on what you enjoy doing most before bedtime. If you love reading, set aside time for this activity at night. It is important to take care of yourself by creating your own morning routine.

Creating your own morning routine will help you get your day started with a positive mindset. There are many ways to get into the mood for the day. For instance, you could read something

Chapter 8: Consistency in business

Consistency is a key component of a successful business. The more consistent you are, the more likely you will be to reach your potential clients or customers.

There are many ways that you can focus on consistency, from building habits to creating structures that help your business run smoothly.

Consistency in your business means that you have a clear vision of your brand, product or service and the way you operate. The first step to achieving consistency is defining your brand values.

Consistency is one of the top marketing strategies for any business because it helps in building trust, gaining loyalty and providing value for customers. It also helps in retaining customers by creating a sense of security and reliability among them.

Businesses should be consistent in their marketing efforts in order to create a brand that is recognizable. The most important part is to ensure that it is not just the external marketing but also the internal one.

The importance of consistency can be seen from different perspectives – economically, psychologically, and even environmentally.

It is the key to success in any business, whether it's personal or professional. Without consistency, there are too many factors that can distract you from your goals and your personal brand.

If you are writing a copy for your online shop, your mission is to help the reader understand what you're about on every page of the website. The best place to start this quest for understanding is with the headline. Why choose a particular word or phrase and how does it tie into other words? What do they imply? These are just a few questions you should ask yourself before writing a headline.

Consistency in your business is one of the most important aspects that you need to focus on. With consistency, your customers know what they can expect from you and your business.

As a business owner, it becomes essential for you to make sure that there is consistency in all aspects of the company's operations - its products, services, and brand values. You also want consistency across all channels that your business operates like social media, advertising campaigns or even website design.

Also, In order to maintain consistency in your online business, your content needs to be relevant and consistent across your website, social media, email marketing, print marketing, etc.

Your content should focus on the target audience of your business. You need to have a clear understanding of what you want them to get from the content. They should find value from it and have a clear call-to-action that tells them what they need to do next.

Consistency in your business is important for establishing trust and maintaining relationships with your customers. It is important to provide the same high quality of service and ensure that you are not missing out on opportunities for your customers.

Again, having a unified brand voice helps you to stay relevant and competitive in today's fast-paced world. It also provides clarity to your customers about who you are and what your business does.

In order to make your business memorable, you need to have a consistent message and be able to communicate it in a clear and concise way.

It is important for a company to have a strong marketing strategy which includes marketing messages, tone of voice, and marketing style.

The consistency in your business will help you develop a brand that customers will find memorable.

Aside from this, we should also be consistent with the way we communicate with our customers. We should provide them with the same information every time they contact us.

We must also make sure that we offer the same value and customer experience to all of our customers and potential customers. It is vital for their satisfaction and trust in your company, which will determine if they will buy from you or not.

A lot of people believe that consistency is one of the most important things when it comes to business.

For many companies, consistency in their marketing is a very important aspect of their brand. If they don't use consistent branding and messaging, they can lose customers and ultimately die out.

An example for this would be the chicken company Kentucky Fried Chicken. They changed their slogan from "Finger-lickin' good" to "We do chicken right" and completely lost their following because of it. This is just one example for why consistency in your business is so important!

A consistent business is one that is able to deliver on promises and keep up a good image. It has a certain level of quality that it delivers every time.

Consistency can be valuable because it provides a sense of trust between the customer and the company. Customers want to know that they will get what they paid for and then some. They want to know that if they buy from you today, they will receive the same service as someone who bought from you yesterday.

Consumers view consistency as a valuable characteristic in their purchase decisions, so it is important to have your business have this trait as well.

Consistency is important for your business because it will also help you to be more successful and it can also help you to grow your customer base. There are many different ways that you can cultivate consistency, but you'll need to know where to start.

An important factor of staying consistent in your business is to be clear on what you want to accomplish. For example, if you want to be an expert in your field, you need to know what that means and how it will look like for the end user.

A lot of entrepreneurs are starting their business with an idea or a product, but they quickly begin to question how they should market themselves. However, if they spend the time upfront understanding their customer and who they are trying to sell their product or service too, it will make it easier for them to create a marketing plan which would bring them success.

Consistency is key to attracting and retaining customers. Customers want to know that they can rely on your business for the same product, service, or experience every time they come back.

To do this, you need to focus on three main areas:

-Brand identity: Your brand needs to establish a consistent personality across all marketing mediums so that your customers know what to expect when they come back for more.

-Product consistency: Your business needs to offer the same product or service at all times so that customers never have to wonder what they might be missing out on. -Customer consistency:

162

You want your customer base to be consistent so that it doesn't fluctuate too much over time. This will help you plan better and increase customer loyalty.

Keep in mind, lack of consistency can lead to many difficulties. In order to keep your company looking professional, it's important to have a consistent voice and tone when communicating with your customers.

You want everything from your marketing material to your customer service interactions to match up in a cohesive manner, so people know what they can expect from you and will continue patronizing your business.

There are many advantages of having consistency in your business. When you follow a set pattern, it becomes easier for people to understand what they can expect from your company.

For example, if your company's M.O is to put out new products on Tuesdays and Fridays, then people will know that the next time they stop by their store or website on Tuesday or Friday, there will be something new waiting for them.

This also helps with marketing because it makes it easier for consumers to remember your brand's image.

It separates you from your competitors, allowing you the time to focus on other parts of your business.

A consistent supply of quality content can be one of the most effective ways to build a business, with it being more important than ever in today's world.

The best way to ensure that you are maintaining consistency is by getting into a routine with your social media posts,(if you are doing online business). By creating a plan for what types of posts you will release on specific days, and then sticking to it, you are able to maintain your schedule without wasting time or resources.

. To be more specific, it's the consistency in your marketing and branding. Your company will always be known for something, and this is what you should focus on when you want to create a distinctive image for your business.

Different businesses will need different marketing strategies in order to stand out and build a strong, recognizable identity. A way of achieving this is by keeping consistency throughout all aspects of business operations - from products and services to the tone of voice in advertising.

There is a misconception that consistency in your marketing is boring or unappealing. On the contrary, it's a major part of what makes a successful business.

Consistency builds trust with your customers and creates familiarity for them. It allows them to keep up with the information you provide, which reduces confusion and makes them feel more comfortable investing in your product or service.

It is crucial to have consistency in your business when it comes to communicating with the customers. Consistency keeps the brand in one place and not scattered in different places.

You have to be consistent with the messaging you want to present in order for your customers to understand what you are trying to sell or offer them. You also have to keep up with the latest trends so that you don't start looking outdated or out of touch with what's happening now.

The simplest way to keep your business consistent is to have a system. This system should be documented so it can be easily understood by anyone in the company. This will allow you to delegate work, anticipate where problems might arise, and streamline your business practices.

Consistency is key to any business. When people choose to follow you, they are looking for familiarity, assurance that they are making the right decision, and peace of mind. Your logo, your colors, your tone of voice, your product descriptions - all need to be the same across channels.

When people see the consistency in your branding on social media or on different channels, it creates trust with them which can lead them onto being loyal customers of yours. The second thing consistency does is help establish credibility with your audience. They will know what to expect from you whenever they see something that features any part of the brand anywhere else online or offline.

If you want your business to succeed, it's important to be consistent in everything that you do. Your products, marketing, design etc. are all integral to the success of your business. You need to make sure that everything aligns with the same vision and gives off the same vibe.

When your marketing is inconsistent with your product or your product is inconsistent with how it was advertised, customers will find these inconsistencies annoying and may not trust in what you are selling. A company needs consistency in order to be successful.

As you start your business, it can be hard to decide what decisions you should make and what format you should use for everything. With a consistent brand, customers are able to understand what they are going to get from the company.

Companies that have a strong message, logo and brand are more likely to have a better customer experience. They are also more likely to generate more revenue.

To achieve consistency in your business, you should also make sure that you have the right marketing tools in place. These include social media platforms, email marketing software and website builder software.

When it comes to your business, consistency can be a key factor in determining its success. This is true even if you don't know what your business is.

As our society becomes more and more reliant on digital services, you should make sure that the way you approach consistency in your business don't hinder its potential.

If we want to succeed as a society, then we need to experiment with new platforms and products that push the boundaries of what's possible.

If you have a small business, you might not need much consistency. You can just keep your marketing strategy and business plan up to date and change things as you go along. But if you're thinking about scaling your business, it's important to establish a framework for how your business will operate in order to determine what changes should be made and how they should be made.

Absolute consistency is almost impossible because things continue to change over time - but this doesn't mean that we shouldn't try our best!

Businesses can benefit from implementing consistency in their business and marketing strategies. Sometimes, the benefits of this are not seen immediately but over time.

Consistency in your business comes with a lot of benefits. It allows you to be more effective, do more work in less time, and even save on costs at the same time.

To impart your brand to everyone who interacts with your company, you need consistency in your company's voice as well as its visual appearance.

Consistency in your business refers to the cohesiveness of how you conduct your business. While consistency is important for every aspect of your business, it is particularly important for building trust and being on the same page with your customers.

Consistency in your business also includes a consistent look and feel across all channels - digital and physical.

This can be achieved by creating standards that are used across your business. When these standards are in place, you can rest assured that your products or services will remain consistent and reliable for your customers.

It is important to maintain consistency in your business from the beginning to the end of the process. Your customers will be more likely to buy from you if they know what to expect each time they make a purchase. By doing this, you give them a sense of security and trustworthiness, which is key for long-term success.

Data and analytics are not the only tools in your toolkit to achieve consistency in your business. As humans, we are naturally inconsistent in our behavior and our thinking--in fact, most of us don't even think about it.

In order to get around this issue, you need to know why people do things and how they can be influenced to change their decisions from one point in time to another point in time.

Consistency in your business goes beyond just having a uniform design for all of your products, services, and marketing materials. It also includes creating a single tone throughout all of your written content. Your brand voice should remain consistent across all platforms from website content to email newsletters to social media posts.

By developing a consistent marketing campaign, you are not only building an image for yourself, but you are also building trust with your customers. It will make your customers feel safer when they purchase from you because they know what to expect from each interaction.

Chapter 9: Consistency is a choice

One of the most difficult choices is how to be consistent in whatever we do in life. The key to becoming consistent is to set yourself up for success by creating a routine, by focusing on what you want and, what you don't want, and also by being persistent.

Whether it's your job or your personal life, consistency will make the difference. For successful individuals, consistency is a choice and not something that is forced upon them. In order for an individual to develop consistency in their life, it takes a lot of hard work and dedication.

Consistency is a choice. You don't have to be consistent but you can choose to be consistent. It takes discipline, dedication and perseverance to stay on the same path no matter what life throws at you.

To be Consistent in whatever we do in life is a choice.

Many people have the same questions in life. Why does it have to be this way? What if I don't like this? What if I could do everything differently and still be happy? The question of what to do and how to feel is one that humans are very confused about.

We tend to do things in our life that we like to do and some activities we enjoy more than others. But those things don't come easily. We need to work for it.

It is not easy to be consistent in what we do in life because it's hard and sometimes too difficult. We might even think of other options, such as taking a break or quitting the activity altogether, but it is important that as long as you are consistent, you will eventually succeed and find satisfaction with what you are doing.

There are many reasons to be consistent in whatever we do in life. We should choose to focus on the right things and be consistent to create a positive impact in our lives.

To be consistent is not always necessary. It is a choice and it can be challenging. The key to being consistent is to understand ourselves and what our purpose is.

Consistency is an important part of our daily lives. It is the desire and need to be consistent in our behavior, attitude, and habits. But how can we maintain a consistent lifestyle in our changing world?

There is no need to be fearful of life's changes since it's how we discover new knowledge and develop. If we attempt to keep an orderly lifestyle could result in becoming rigid and rigid, that can result in stagnation.

The author is of the opinion that consistency is a decision must be made. But what is the distinction between being driven consistently by the same principles or values?

The ability to be consistent with what you do is a decision. It's up to us to decide if we are going to be conscientious and how we would like to tackle the job.

It's been said that it is essential to be a person of regularity, but are truly willing to make the work? Yes, we are. Consistency is essential to avoid negative outcomes like boredom, ruts and tension.

Consistency can be both personal and common. Consistency for the individual is the decision to lead an existence that is alignment with your goals to become. Many people wish to maintain their consistency in order to stay true to who they are and fulfill their mission.

For you to make sure your lifestyle is consistent, take a look at these questions:

What is my goal in my life?

- What goals do I have?

What's most important to me?

What do I do with my time?

What happens If I do the same thing time?

Being consistent with everything it is that we do in our lives is a personal choice. Not being consistent can be a decision too. What is the best way to force one person remain consistently? This is the question that can be answered with these:

What is it that will make them feel secure and at ease

What are their motives to change?

Can they sustain consistency? they to maintain consistency?

If they're dissatisfied with the uniformity and consistency, what would they like and how can they achieve that?

In order to be constant in everything life brings us the main factor is to be conscious of what you are looking for and the way you'd like to appear and it's a decision.

What's the point of remaining consistent in all that you do?

Consistency with what we do will create a sense of stability and predictability within our lives. When a person feels an underlying sense of order and predictability, they'll be more efficient and more efficient.

It has also been proven to boost happiness levels, which are needed by people to feel when struggling with finding out what they ought to do in their lives.

A lot of times we do not think about the things that make us feel happy or happy. We focus on the things that are practical and effective.

Life is full of various things we perform just to do these things. As an example, we take breakfast every morning and make sure to put on our shoes prior to leaving. So, the question is whether it a choice, or a requirement? must do?

It's crucial to keep in mind that we are innately designed to follow through with the things we are doing in the world. You can't decide for that one day we'll stop eating breakfast and not wearing shoes when necessary.

Consistency is one of the qualities is something we must always seek out. It assists us in keeping our brain in the best condition and can assist us in being more efficient.

What's important to be constant is to come up with an action plan and then executing it, and lastly, obtaining the support of those who are around your. It can be an arduous goal to reach, however it's worthwhile after you've accomplished your goal.

The ability to be consistent in everything you do is a decision. It doesn't matter if it's something minor or large, it's the decision of us to follow through or not.

It's crucial that we do not make decision lightly and think about the benefits from being consistent. First, we must consider the longer-term effects being inconsistent could have on us.

Most people believe that the success we achieve in whatever you do is due to our perseverance in what we perform. But, this isn't the case. Our achievements are actually an outcome of our ability to carry on doing the things we're good in.

For this to be achieved it is essential to take a balanced view of how they utilize their energy and time. If, for instance, you are looking to remain constant in your behavior, then you must have the ability to apply all of your energy into what it is that you have to do with no doubt.

Human nature is to be inconstant. It is not easy to stay in the same place regarding the goals we set and our priorities. For my private life, I would like to remain consistent with everything I do, such as exercise, eating healthy as well as keeping up to date with my professional advancement.

In the work environment We believe we must be productive, day in and day out and not be tardy for a meeting or due date. The result is burning out due to procrastination, exhaustion and fatigue due to tension.